# THE FUTURE IS NOW

*How Elon Musk Is Shaping A Better Tomorrow*

# CONTENTS

# INTRODUCTION

Congratulations on downloading *The Future Is Now: How Elon Musk Is Shaping A Better Tomorrow* and thank you for doing so. While you have likely only started to hear his name relatively recently, Elon Musk has been on the bleeding edge of most of the major technological advancements in the past 25 years. In addition to sending his car into space, he also holds a majority share in the largest solar company in California, helped to invent the payment service that many people likely used to buy this book and much more.

While all of these achievements are certainly noteworthy, they aren't why Elon Musk deserves to have countless books like this one written about him. No, that fact comes from his innate desire to make the human race better, to see them treat the planet in a more sustainable fashion and to help them literally spread out amongst the stars. With such lofty goals, is there any reason that there are plenty of life lessons than Musk has to offer as well?

As such, the following chapters will start with an overview

of Musk's accomplishments, before then discussing his tumultuous childhood and the machinations that saw this South African youth attending college in Canada and ultimately reaching his goal of living in the United States. Next, we will follow Musk as he works his way through his first few companies from Zip2 to X.com. You will then find chapters that discuss each of his modern pursuits in detail including SpaceX, Tesla Motors and side projects such as OpenAI and Hyperloop.

From there you will find a discussion of the many positive qualities that Musk exudes that anyone would do well to follow if they hoped to have even a fraction of his overall success. Finally, you will learn a little about Musk in his own words with excerpts from several speeches he has given over the years.

There are plenty of books on this subject on the market, thanks again for choosing this one! Every effort was taken to ensure it is full of as much useful information as possible, please enjoy!

# CHAPTER 1.

# MEET ELON MUSK

While, for most of the world, Elon Musk was their first introduction to the Musk family line, for those in South Africa the name has a fair amount of cultural cache. As such, the future visionary spent his childhood hearing stories about his grandparents who were the first people to fly between Australia and Africa in an airplane. He also heard plenty of stories about his great-grandfather who won a famous race across the length of Africa and another grandmother who was the first woman in Canada to hold a chiropractor's license. With such a distinguished lineage, is it any wonder that the Musk family has always seen themselves as adventurers?

This mentality is something that the current Musk has taken to heart and has worked to embody virtually his entire life. In his first fifty years, he has had a hand in creating one of the most ubiquitous services on the internet, revitalized the space program, helped to make electric cars mainstream, created an entirely new type of highspeed travel and more. Despite not being American, Musk is a true modern example of the American dream.

A self-made man, Musk worked his way through college and started a business that took advantage of the burgeoning technology that was the internet that then became so successful that he became a millionaire before he was 30. Instead of resting on his laurels and taking up permanent residence on a beach somewhere, Musk reinvested his earnings in a new company that would ultimately go on to be synonymous with paying for things on the internet.

When PayPal was purchased by eBay, this left Musk with four times his already substantial net worth and more time on his hands than he knew what to do with. He still wasn't satisfied, however, and sunk all of his holdings into multiple technologies that he felt confident would affect the future in a big way. This is what ultimately lead him to the place in the spotlight that he holds today with a leading role in both Tesla Motors and SpaceX. Along the way, he also ended up owning a major share in one of the largest solar power companies in California. Then, literally in his spare time, he and his team created what could soon be the future of long-distance travel in what is known as the Hyperloop.

Musk still isn't done, however, which is why, in his free time, he is working with a nonprofit organization he started to ensure that when artificial intelligence is finally unleashed on the world in a big way that it will benefit humanity as a whole as opposed to attempting to reduce it to a smoldering crater the way practically every permutation on that story humanity has ever created says it will. What it comes down to, is that if there is a slightly futuristic technology that is sure to make the world a better place in the long run, then there is a safe bet that Musk is heavily invested in some type of business or organization that is working to make it a reality.

## Key personality traits

While undeniably of genius level intelligence, this is only a boon to Musk's other talents, not the source of them. No, his greatest strength comes with his ability to look at the big picture and to determine the most profitable options related to whatever the current course of action may be. This, in turn, is a facet of his ability to quickly absorb vast amounts of new information and then be able to utilize it properly at a moment's notice.

This can most clearly be seen during the time he spent

getting SpaceX up and running by first reading everything he could about space travel and then getting a group of rocket scientists together and asking them every question he could think of. After literally teaching himself rocket science he was then able to accurately predict the market for such things as he understood where it was likely going in the future.

With this unique blend of foresight, intellect, and business prowess, Musk could do literally anything he wanted. If he lived in a comic book universe he would have already put his mind to donning a cowl and fighting crime. While he would not seem out of place standing next to the likes of Bruce Wayne or Tony Stark, we are all lucky that he is real, and he is spectacular.

# CHAPTER 2.

# EARLY LIFE

Elon Musk has always been an engineer and a business person at heart. He has always been an avid reader, and as a child he would read 10 hours a day. He read through his entire local library and when they ran out of books he went ahead and just read the complete Encyclopedia Britannica.

At some point in his young life, he took up an interest in programming. It's quite possible that this could have been because his father was an engineer. Even if his father had nothing to do with it, it was definitely possible because of Elon's high intelligence. He took a six-month course in BASIC. It was obviously too slowly paced for him because he finished it in just 3 days. When he was 12, he used his newfound programming knowledge to write a very simple computer game called Blastar. The code for the game was published in a magazine and he was paid $500 for it. Years later, the game was remade as a HTML5 game. Elon Musk was quoted as saying "[It was] a trivial game... but better than Flappy Bird."

Despite this early success, Musk's childhood was far from perfect and, like many children who are small for their age, he was regularly bullied across the numerous private schools he attended during these years. By middle school, the bullying had grown so severe that he was actually hospitalized after a particularly brutal attack.

By the time he was a teenager, the country of South Africa was in the midst of a serious conflict over the topic of Apartheid. As a citizen, once he finished school he would be required to fulfill his mandatory time in the military which meant that he would then be forced to spend his time silencing those who were speaking out against this racist practice. His first choice for escape was the United States, where he was interested in becoming a part of the nascent computer technology scene, but he failed to gain access to the country despite his best efforts.

As he was not one to take failure lying down, Musk thought outside the box and decided to instead go to Canada, where he had citizenship from his mother's side. At the age of 18, he went to live with his family in Canada and started working odd jobs. While he had successfully avoided actively supporting racism, his overall position had not improved all that much as his family could provide a roof over his head but little else. He took every odd job he could find but remained relatively destitute as he saved every penny he could to afford tuition at a local college.

He wasn't picky about the type of work he picked up either, regularly taking jobs no one else wanted including things like picking vegetables, shoveling grain and even cleaning out the boiler room at the local saw mill. This was a job that was perpetually open as no one ever managed to handle it for any real length of time.

While Musk was confident that he could withstand just about anything, he quickly learned just what it was he was up against. The job required him to wear a full hazmat suit, while cleaning the boiler itself required him to cram himself into a tight dark space for hours at a time. To make things even worse, parts of the boiler could unexpectedly remain hotter than anticipated at unpredictable times so the risk of injury was high. Despite the danger, Musk persevered far longer than most on the job and was able to save enough to pay for a tuition to college the following year.

Musk first attended Queens University in Ontario where he

studied for two years. In his spare time, he would spend time with mother and younger brother Kimbal who had come to live in Canada in the interim. Together, Musk and his brother would read the newspaper and then take turns calling the people they read about in an effort to get them to agree to have lunch. One local person of interest they spoke with was a bank president. Their meeting so impressed the man that he offered Musk an internship and an invitation to his daughter's birthday party. When questioned about the party, the bank manager's daughter can still remember the conversation she had with Musk, it was about how he thought there should be a greater worldwide focus on electric cars.

## Moving to the US

By 1992, Musk had impressed more than local celebrities, his stellar grades were enough to earn him a scholarship to the University of Pennsylvania and granting him the access to the United States that he was still aiming for. He also continued his entrepreneurship while in college, where he sold computers out of his dorm room and ran a speakeasy.

In 1993 and 1994, he received back to back bachelor's degrees, first in physics and then in economics. Despite his academic success, during this time Musk also found himself battling severe depression as he struggled with the idea of what to do next. To find the answer he studied the work of countless philosophers as well as prominent religious texts. While all of this work helped him to better understand his question, the one that provided him with the answers he sought was *The Hitchhiker's Guide to the Galaxy* by Douglas Adams.

For those who are unfamiliar, at one point in the story, the main character asks another character, who is in a position to know what the meaning of life is. This question is answered with a matter of fact "42" before the story moves on. While most of those who read this back and forth likely took it as a joke, this answer struck Musk in a profound way. He has since explained that this passage taught him the importance of not just asking the right question but asking it at the right time. At the time, young Musk thought about the meaning of life for a while before then considering what the right question would be to ask in his current situation.

After giving his situation some thought, Musk decided that the best question to ask at the current moment would be, "What technologies are likely going to have the greatest overall effect on the human race as a whole in the near future." After then giving the question some thought, his answers were the internet, space travel and renewable energy. With his questions answered, Musk considered which of these industries offered the most promise to start, with the lowest required startup costs, and settled on the internet. This in turn led him to decide to move to California so he applied to Stanford University for a graduate program where he was supposedly going to study physics.

While this has never been confirmed publicly, it is widely believed that Musk applied to Stanford so that he could renew his student visa for another year while at the same time taking advantage of the funds that the school provided to finance his move. Whatever his reasons, Musk waited a whole two days into the new school year before dropping out to form his first company known as Zip2. It took less than four years for him to become a millionaire.

# CHAPTER 3.

# EARLY DAYS

## Zip2

Before heading out to California, Musk spent much of his time watching in awe as Netscape Communications went public, turning a man younger than himself into a millionaire overnight. At this time his net worth totaled about $2,000 and a used car but he already had an idea of what he was going to next and how he was going to make his plan a reality.

Zip2 was a company that started off by providing local businesses an internet presence. Later, they sold city guide information to local newspapers. As the story goes, in 1995, Elon Musk and his brother, Kimbal, started Zip2 with a small loan from their father as well as angel investors. However, Musk later said he didn't receive any money from his father. They rented an office where they ran and built Zip2. In order to save money, they both lived out of the office they were renting. As if that wasn't hard enough, they only had one computer between the two of them. That computer was used for both programming and as a server for the company website. The brothers would leave the computer on during the day to run the website. Then they would take it down at night so that Elon could program and maintain the website all night long. They didn't even have their own phone line to use for an internet connection and instead drilled a hole in the floor to plug into the system of the restaurant downstairs.

The service was created after Musk met the creators of the digital mapping company Navteq and convinced them to allow him access to their online maps. With this promise in hand, he then purchased a directory of businesses in his area before digitizing it and adding a little bit of code to combine the two. The end result was one of the first all-digital mapping services to be available online.

With a unique, functioning product in hand, Musk was soon able to secure meetings with major newspapers. He then advertised his success on the pages that his clients were paying for and interest skyrocketed. During this time, Musk worked 7 days a week and almost never left the office. Somehow though, he briefly managed to have a girlfriend during this time. And for 3 months, if she ever wanted to see him, she had to visit him at the office.

In 1996 Zip2 raised 3 million dollars in investment money. Shortly after the investment, the investors kicked Musk out of the CEO position and made him CTO instead. They believed that a traditional business executive named Richard Sorkin would be a more natural fit for the job, largely because of his degree from Sanford. The irony was not lost on Musk, but there was little he could do as the expansion of the company started off strong as Sorkin landed a number of major contracts with newspapers from around the country.

Contrary to the way Musk had always run the company, Sorkin then began to double dip on his customer base, taking advertising revenue from the very newspapers they were already providing service to. This felt like the final straw to Musk, but he owned less than 10 percent of the stock of his former company so there was nothing he could do while other services like Yahoo! And MapQuest moved into the space while his company languished in the past, now tied to the companies it was supposed to treat as clients.

By the end of 1996, stuck in a vice president role, Musk learned that Sorkin was getting ready to sell Zip2 to a company called CitySearch that was hoping to beat Google to the punch. This was the line in the sand for Musk as if he didn't step up then and there he knew he would have very little left to fight for at all. As such, he spread the word of his plan throughout the company before publicly staging a revolt to have Sorkin removed from his position. As a majority of the big names at the company were behind him, the board caved and gave Sorkin the boot.

While this seemed like a victory for Musk at first, things slipped away from him at the last minute, as the board was now made up largely of members of the old guard who liked where Sorkin was taking the company. As such, they put Derek Proudian, formerly of Mohr Davidow, into the CEO position. By 1998, Zip2 had gone nationwide and provided services to more than 160 newspapers, including the *New York Times*. By this time Zip2 was providing calendars, email and more to newspapers. In 1999, Zip2 was bought by Compaq Computer. Musk received $22 million from the sale of Zip2, which was purchased for $300 million, the most any online company had ever been purchased for at that time. The company was then folded into the larger Compaq infrastructure and there was no room left in his company for Musk.

At the time, Musk was critical of the sale noting that the venture capital firm should have left him in charge as "Great things never happen with professional managers or VCs [venture capitalist firms] in charge, they don't have the insight or the creativity."

Despite its overall success, Musk has always personally considered Zip2 a failure due to the fact that when creating it he was hoping to have a hand in more actively shaping the internet as a whole. If he had had his way, it seems, things would have developed with more of an active eye out for the consumer about anything else. Likewise, the fact that he created a way for a dying industry to remain relevant for a handful of additional years stuck with him which is why his next venture was designed from the group up to challenge the status quo at every turn.

## X.com

By 1999, Musk was getting ready to pitch a brand-new idea, an online financial services platform that worked without a need for any type of traditional financial services provider. He took his pitch to Sequoia Capital a well-known firm that the likes of Oracle, Cisco and Apple had all used to get their start. That same day he walked out of the meeting with $25 million in investment capital for his next venture, a website known as X.com.

The pitch that Musk gave to Sequoia would sound familiar to anyone who uses PayPal on a regular basis. However, the version of the website that launched in 1999 was a bare bones affair that was exclusively focused on handling person-to-person transactions, something that had never been done online up to that point.

While the company saw some traction in its first year, its overall value was still in its potential. A company called Confinity saw this potential and offered to purchase the company whole cloth while still leaving Musk in charge of the entire affair. Confinity had a product that allowed PDA users to send money to each other through infrared ports. Elon Musk was interested in the prospect of transferring money electronically. After the two companies merged, they considered X.com to be a better name than Confinity. However, they did a study and learned that people found X.com to be vague and quite possibly pornographic, so they changed the name to PayPal.

While the two companies worked well together on paper, the same could not be said for the teams of people that made each company worth investing in the first place. As such, instead of moving forward with the new PayPal software in any real way, Musk spent much of the next year simply struggling to keep a wide variety of conflicting personalities, egos and visions inline as best he could.

This wasn't what Confinity founders Peter Thiel and Max Levchin were looking for when they agreed to let Musk be CEO, however, and the next year when Musk left the country to meet with new investors Levchin and Thiel used his absence to dispose him from his position as CEO. The control of the company then reverted fully to Confinity who sold it to eBay the next year for roughly $1.5 billion split between eBay stock and cold hard cash. Despite being ousted from yet another company, Musk still owned more than 10 percent of PayPal's stock which means the sale left him with more than $150 million in cash and stock options.

PayPal has continued to grow over the years. It went public in 2002 and was bought by eBay later that year. After being tightly tied to eBay for several years, eBay made PayPal its own company in 2015.

As of today, PayPal has 218 million active accounts. And it trades money in 25 different currencies. PayPal is used globally by businesses, individuals, and charities. It lets people send money to relatives all over the world. It has let parents set up spending accounts on debit cards for college students to teach students about financial responsibility. PayPal provides a line of credit and even an ATM-like card. PayPal has a service called PayPal. Me that allows people to send money through text or email without even needing a PayPal account. PayPal also provides payment solutions for small businesses.

It turns out that Elon Musk was right about PayPal and the future of digital finance. PayPal has completely revolutionized the way that people spend money and make purchases online. They've managed to do all of this without actually ever being a bank.

# CHAPTER 4.

# SPACEX

After selling PayPal, Elon Musk had a few million dollars burning a hole in his pocket. He thought it would be a good idea to spark public interest in space exploration by sending something small, like maybe a mouse, into outer space. He didn't have the ambition to build a rocket at that time because he will still under the mistaken impression that it would be cheaper just to buy one.

Musk has always been extremely vocal when it comes to his thoughts on space travel and the long-term survival of mankind. In fact, he has been quoted as saying that he wants to die on Mars, just not on impact. As such, before he had even received the funds from the PayPal buyout he was already working on something that would eventually become the Mars Oasis project. The goal of this project is to launch a remote-controlled greenhouse into space and have it land on Mars where it would then be ready for any colonization project that may then develop.

Musk's goals for this project were twofold, first it would help with potential terraforming efforts to promote the growth of the human race, and second, it would revitalize interest in the flagging space program, making number one that much more likely to happen. Musk's broader goals are then to ensure the survival of the human race in the long-term by ensuring it spreads out among the stars before some type of extinction level event comes along and wipes out all the progress that has been made in the past few thousand years.

His first attempt involved a trip to Paris with his partners Adeo Ressi and Jim Cantrell. They thought the European space company Ariana space would be able to sell them rockets but found that they were much too expensive. During that meeting, though they found out that the Russians wanted to offload some repurposed ICBM missiles, so, Musk and his partners went to Russia.

While in Russia, they got much more than they were expecting. They had to pay off corrupt cops on the road to their meeting. When they finally got to the Russian negotiations, they involved drinking a lot of vodka. They got the distinct impression that the entire Russian space program was fueled by vodka. When they went into the meeting room, each Russian had a bottle of vodka in front of him. They toasted once every couple of minutes. By the end of the meeting, all three of the Americans had passed out drunk on the table.

After returning home Musk and Ressi, were approached by the Russians and told that negotiations couldn't continue unless the Russians were given $5,000 in cash. The Americans paid them off. During the third meeting, the Americans went back to Russia. They were ready to purchase three ICBM missiles for $21 million. They were disappointed to realize that the Russians now wanted that amount for each rocket. When Elon Musk debated the price, the Russians tease him. They said, "Oh, little boy, you don't have the money?"

On the flight back, Elon Musk said to Cantrell, "I think we can build a rocket ourselves." And that's exactly what he did. In 2002, he built SpaceX with his own money. After running the numbers, Musk realized that not only would it be cheaper to start his own company that manufactures rockets, but also that he could make a profit selling them to governments around the world who were interested in rockets of their own.

It turns out, the companies that were then making rockets charged an astronomical markup on their costs, so much so that one percent of the sale price could legitimately be enough to cover all of the costs accrued during construction. As such, he could lower the prices of the rockets a whole fifty percent, corner the market and still turn a profit while hardly even trying. As an added bonus, Musk figured that owning his own company would make it far easier to tweak the design of the rockets they produced to ensure they were as likely to make it to Mars as possible.

After that Elon Musk gathered a collection of some of the smartest people in the industry. As much as he understood about rocket science, he knew that he couldn't understand everything. Elon Musk knew where to draw the line and respected that other people had greater knowledge in certain areas than he did. Musk would also really listen to people and gained a lot of knowledge from them as well.

It's been asked, "How did Elon Musk get started learning about Rockets?" He had 2 degrees in both physics and economics. However, those degrees aren't rocket science. And they didn't give him nearly enough information necessary to run a commercial spaceflight company.

Elon Musk contacted Jim Cantrell, a consultant for the Aerospace industry. Jim Cantrell later became the first vice president of Business Development for SpaceX. He also became Elon Musk's mentor as well as a consultant.

Cantrell said that Elon Musk used a 2-part learning system. First off, he committed textbooks to memory. Cantrell loaned Elon Musk a handful of books just to get him started. The books were "Aerothermodynamics of Gas Turbine and Rocket Propulsion," "Rocket Propulsion Elements," "International Reference Guide to Space Launch Systems," and "Fundamentals of Astrodynamics." You know, the basics.

The second part was that Musk built a network of the smartest people. As much as Elon Musk new, he was aware that he didn't know everything. That's why he gathered around him the absolute brightest in the industry. Elon Musk showed the scientists and his network the utmost respect. And he would listen to those people as well. However, it didn't just go in one ear and out the other, he learned a lot more from every one of those people. That in turn, let him be able to hold a conversation about profoundly technical topics with any of them.

By 2006, SpaceX had built and launched its first rocket. It exploded. By 2007 SpaceX launched its second rocket. It exploded as well. In 2008 SpaceX tried again and launched its third rocket. The third rocket, named Falcon 1, was carrying several satellites. One of the satellites belonged to the Pentagon, and two of them belonged to NASA. There was also a micro-laboratory called Presat onboard. The third rocket exploded spectacularly. As bad as it was, each of these rockets made it further than the one before.

Musk was asked about his third SpaceX failure in a row on *60 minutes.* "Did you think I need to pack this in?" To which, Elon Musk, without a moment's hesitation said "Never." "Why not?" "I don't ever give up. I'd have to be dead or completely incapacitated." Eight weeks later he launched one more flight that could have cost him the company. SpaceX did not have the resources to launch the fifth flight. This fourth launch was a success.

In 2008, SpaceX won a contract from NASA to provide commercial resupply services worth $1.6 billion. This contract was meant to secure the ability to resupply the International Space Station after the shuttle was retired. The contract required that SpaceX deliver 12 flights to the space station. This helped cement the future of SpaceX. By this time the rockets that SpaceX was designing were a full 90 percent cheaper than their competition while at the same time maintaining an average profit margin of more than 70 percent.

There have always been significant problems with space travel. First off, it requires massive amounts of energy to propel an object into orbit. On top of that, any payload added to that object increases the weight and therefore requires more energy. That energy comes in the form of rocket fuel, which is extremely expensive. There is another challenge with Rocket Fuel, and that is that it adds to the weight. So, the more rocket fuel you have, the more rocket fuel you need to launch a rocket into space.

In the past, Rockets have been built in such a way that they would burn off fuel, then dispose of the part of the rocket that contained that fuel once it had been spent. Then the rocket would burn more fuel from the next part, or stage and dispose of that. Those pieces of the rocket are also extremely expensive. They require thousands of hours to engineer and build.

In order to solve the problem of reusable parts, the space shuttle was invented. The space shuttle was a craft that was designed to be reusable, so it could be sent into space over and over again. However, the space shuttle was not without its faults as well. The space shuttle also had to dispose of fuel during its launch. And once the space shuttle returned to the ground, it still took thousands of man-hours to ready it for the next flight. Those man-hours also cost a lot of money. So, while the space shuttle was an improvement from rockets, it was still far from perfect.

In order to get SpaceX up and running, Musk spent nearly $90 million of his own money because he believed it was the right thing to do for humanity as a whole. This is why SpaceX's motto is "make humanity a spacefaring race".

Since its inception, SpaceX has generated a pair of unmanned launch vehicles, Falcon 1 and Falcon 9, as well as a fully functioning unmanned spacecraft christened Dragon. Falcon 1 was the first vehicle that had even made it to orbit using liquid fuel and launched by a private company when it had its first flight in 2009. In 2012, NASA signed a contract with SpaceX to put Dragon solely in charge of refueling the international space station as well as delivering the astronauts supplies from the surface. Dragon is now used instead of the actual space shuttle for space flights which means Musk reinvented space travel in less than 20 years.

This is only the first of SpaceX's many successes, however, as the company also launched its first satellite into orbit in 2013, with a second in 2015 following it up by being built to observe deep space directly. SpaceX is also in the midst of working out the logistics surrounding a project known as Starlink that, among other things, will involve the launch of around 4,000 satellites that would theoretically ensure that everyone in the world has ready access to fast, reliable internet. The details surrounding just what these satellites will entail is being kept under wraps, but the first round of prototypes is due to be launched in February 2018. A spokesperson from the company indicated during a meeting with Congress last year that if the early tests go well, the first round of operational satellites could be ready to launch as early as 2019.

At the same time, the company outlined its plans to have the project fully up and running by no later than 2024. Unlike some of Musk's other projects, this one doesn't seem to on track to be a charitable act, and instead will likely be the cash cow that provides the funds for Musk's ultimate goal of building a city on Mars. The cost of the project is reported to be about $10 billion, which means the profits are likely going to be substantial to justify the tremendous cost.

All told, SpaceX is the most prolific creators of rocket engines bar none. The Merlin 1D model engine is powerful enough to lift over 40 cars and is currently being put to use around the world for more mundane purposes as well. SpaceX received more than $2 billion in federal funding to get the Merlin 1A working correctly and this grant directly led to the ultimate success of both the Dragon and the Falcon.

## Falcon Heavy

SpaceX launched the Falcon Heavy rocket in February 2018, the most powerful rocket ever built, putting the company yet another step closer to its eventual goal of Mars colonization. The Heavy is a heavy-lift partially-reusable launch vehicle with the ability for its side boosters to return to earth after launching their payload. It is based on the original Falcon 9 design with additional boosters to account for the additional weight of its payloads which could include things like telescopes, national security satellites, and even Mars Oasis habitats if the mood strikes them.

All told it contains 27 different engines, more than any other working rocket has ever gotten off the ground. This, in turn, provides it with more than 5 million pounds of thrust and allows it to carry approximately 140,000 pounds at once, more than twice what its competition can carry. What's more impressive still, is that it is more powerful than the new rocket that NASA is working on, while still being fully functional at just about one-tenth the cost. As an added bonus, having a cheaper rocket in play will likely make additional missions to the moon possible, something that Musk surely appreciates. It also coincides nicely with the late 2017 presidential mandate that America return to the moon and even makes it an economically feasible option.

While its first successful launch wasn't until 2018, the plans for the Heavy have been underway since 2011 when SpaceX refurbished a launch complex at the Vandenberg Air Force Base with the goal being a 2013 launch. This date was ultimately pushed back, however after the failure that the company experienced in June 2013. This was then followed by a series of setbacks that ultimately pushed the launched back from 2016, all the way to 2018.

In July 2017, during an International Space Station research and development meeting, Musk downplayed the maiden voyage of the Heavy saying that he would consider the initial launch a success as long as the rocket didn't do any direct damage to the launch pad. The payload for this initial launch was Musk's own midnight cherry Roadster, along with a mannequin wearing sunglasses, a sign that says, "don't panic" (a nod to *Hitchhiker's Guide to the Galaxy)* and David Bowie's Space Oddity playing on loop via solar power. It will make it as far as Mar's orbit, where presumably Musk will stop and pick it up, so he has some wheels to tool around Mars when he gets there himself.

There was something else inside the Roadster however. It is a type of storage file storage system, known as an Arch. It is designed to keep its data retrievable for millions of years across the harshest environments and even in the void of space. It is also about the size of a quarter and looks like a quartz mini-disc. So, what did Musk put on this disk? The completely *Foundation* trilogy by Isaac Asimov, his other main inspiration.

After its successful maiden voyage, Falcon Heavy already has two additional flights scheduled for this year with another planned for 2019. Additionally, there are rumors circulating that it will also take a pair of very rich and very lucky tourists on a personal trip around the moon. One flight of the Heavy, assuming all of its pieces make it back to earth in one piece, costs $90 million, which sounds like a lot until you learn that the system that NASA currently uses for the services the Heavy can provide typically costs about $1 billion per flight.

## What it all means

Before first coming up with the idea for the Mars Oasis project, Musk didn't know anything more about jet propulsion than anyone else, much less the specifics that ensures one is legitimately well-versed in rocket science. In order to solve this problem, he simply befriended some local rocket scientists and asked to borrow the research they had lying around. When one of the scientists asked what research he meant, Musk simply picked a bookcase at random and gestured to all of it. It was only after he was well-versed enough in the topic to understand the basics that he was able to go out and hire the types of scientists that would help him make his dream into a reality.

It is important to keep in mind that this was the level of commitment and dedication that Musk put into the project when he was still just planning on buying a Russian rocket for a one-off mission. Nevertheless, during this phase, he was already brainstorming ideas of his own and consulting with his rocket scientists on the plan that would ultimately lead to Falcon 1, the first rocket ship his team built which he named in honor of the Millennium Falcon.

Other inspirations that Musk has drawn on over the years include the Isaac Asimov series *Foundation* and he has cited Asimov as a serious influence when it comes to the correct application for space travel technology in the near future. Musk has also pointed out that it has taken humanity about as long to develop reliable space travel as it originally did for them to crawl out of the primordial ooze. In his opinion, it is just about time for a serious upheaval.

It is also important to keep in mind that creating the most successful rocket manufacturing company on the planet was only Musk's secondary goal. The whole purpose of the original trip to Russia, remember, was to make space travel a realistic goal for humanity again. The Mars Oasis project is actually just the first step in a much larger project that will likely see a manned mission to Mars in the next 15 years and hopes to have 100,000 people living on the Red Planet by 2040.

What's more, to exactly no one's surprise, Musk has already gone on record numerous times as saying that his colony on Mars is going to be all electric, all the time. As another facet of this project, he has also created the Musk Foundation whose entire goal is to consider the various clean or renewable energy sources that can ultimately be used to make space travel more efficient, safer, cheaper and faster. If things continue apace, then when the first round of human settlers get to Mars, they will find Musk there to greet them and shake each of their hands personally. That or take them for a ride in his Roadster. After all, who doesn't like David Bowie?

# CHAPTER 5.

# TESLA MOTORS

While Musk was busying himself working on transportation to the stars, another group of engineers was working on a prototype for what would ultimately become the Tesla Roadster. As he had already been thinking a lot about electric cars for more than 20 years at this point, Musk was happy to jump in with funding as soon as he first heard about the project. He took on the position of chairman of the board at the time of the first round of public funding. This position allowed him to take on a dramatically expanded role when it came time for the first commercially released product in the line, the Tesla Roadster.

While the number of cars that it boasts on the road is relatively small, the automotive industry is already referring to it as the modern Ford Company based on its potential to disrupt the existing automotive infrastructure. It is also worth pointing out that it is the first new automotive company that has been launched in the United

States for more than 100 years.

While certainly a part of the Roasters final design, Musk didn't take on an active management role in the company until 2008, right around the start of the Great Recession. He became CEO around this time, as well as taking on the position of lead project architect. While the product line has since gone on to be a great success, its creation was anything but a smooth experience.

Martin Eberhard and Marc Tarpenning, the creators of the prototype Tesla that caught Musk's eye, first met Musk in 2001 when they went to hear him speak as part of a symposium on space travel. They exchanged pleasantries and nothing much came of the encounter except that Musk remembered their names when they met again three years later in 2004 to pitch Musk on the idea for an electric car called the TZero.

Musk was instantly intrigued by their proposal and arranged to meet with the pair soon after to try the car for himself. What was scheduled as a quick 30-minute drive around the block soon expanded to more than three hours as the group discussed everything about the TZero and the broader importance of creating a vehicle that could compete with the current automotive offerings while still being truly energy efficient. This meeting also led to the ultimate rollout of the Tesla strategy of a high-end model first to capture the minds of the public before the introduction of a more economic model that would be capable of actually changing the way that the public thought about electric cars.

The original version of the plan wasn't without its own flaws as well, however, as it saw the first Tesla Roadster rolling off the assembly line in 2006 so the company would easily be turning a profit by 2008. This timeline ended up being almost completely unrealistic, however, and it became just the first thing that Musk and Eberhard butted heads over as the creation of the Roaster languished behind one production or engineering problem after the next.

This was largely due to the fact that it was during this period that Musk took on a more hands-on role in the design of the vehicle, making changes to the core design including things like moving the placement of the doors and insisting that the company create its own unique headlights as well. These changes caused the timeline to increase substantially, with further delays ultimately mounting as the decision came down to redesign the seats, the interior as a whole and even the transmission itself from virtually the ground up. While these changes would ultimately serve to ensure that the original Roadster would have a quality to match its premium price tag, it pushed the tight production schedule well past the breaking point.

As many of the parts that were ultimately used for the Roadster were completely unique, it put the company in the position of sourcing unique parts, which was a task that no one who worked for the company at the time was even remotely equipped to do. This, in turn, led to Musk taking on an additional role in the company and visiting the Lotus manufacturing plant in England that the company was working with to create the Roadster in an effort to get a better handle on the continuously spiraling production deadline and cost. Through all of this Musk stuck to his guns, as is his way, and ultimately ended up being the primary creative force behind the final result.

In 2007, more than a year behind their initial plan and still years from being profitable, Musk and Eberhard got into a particularly heated argument over an article where Musk was credited with the creation of the vehicle while Eberhard wasn't mentioned at all. Eberhard left the company soon after amidst a flurry of allegations over lawsuits over everything from breach of contract to slander.

At this point Musk took on the duties of CEO, making his first act in the position to fire a quarter of the existing staff as the protracted production schedule meant the company was hemorrhaging money and it was the only way to ensure his $50 million investment wasn't going to become a huge mistake.

One interesting fact, despite having been in existence for more than a decade, Tesla Motors was only able to acquire the URL Tesla.com in 2016. Before this time, it was held by a man named Stuart Grossman who had been holding onto the domain since Musk had been with PayPal. While Grossman wasn't using the domain for anything particularly relevant, he planned to continue holding it, just in case, until a personal visit from Musk changed his mind. While the price that caused the domain to change hands was not disclosed, those close to Musk say that he would have easily paid $5 million to secure it once and for all.

## Vindication...eventually

In 2008, with the first Tesla Roadsters rolling off the line, Musk should have been basking in the glow of his success. Instead, the early reviews were terrible to middling. From there, the initial Roadster run continued to be plagued with a host of problems, so much so that by 2010 more than three-quarters of all of the series one Roadsters on the market had been recalled for one reason or another. The initial run of the Roadster ended after just 2,150 units were produced and shipped to more than 20 countries around the world.

As before when an early version of an idea didn't work out according to plan, Musk was nonplussed by the rocky start and simply decided that the first run had just been a field test that verified a concept that was sound, if in need of some additional fine-tuning. As he is want to do in these situations, Musk doubled down on his investment in Tesla and started taking preorders for the second-generation Roadster called the Roadster Model S.

Contrary to the early reviews of the original Roadster, the reviews of the Model S were extremely positive. So much so that the company was able to ride the wave of good publicity to an initial public offering worth more than $100 million. This amount was about twice what Musk had invested in the company so far. The company was worth about $25 billion in 2016 and worth about twice that at the start of 2018 on the verge of the release of the Model 3. None of this is enough for Musk, however, who believes that his company will be worth 15 times that before 2030.

After the Model S launched to significantly improved reviews and started taking off in the way that Musk and the other creators had envisioned all those years before, Tesla Motors introduced a 4-door variation of the Model S and their first electric sports utility vehicle, the Model X. The company has also begun to manufacture the power train system that drives the current electric offerings from Toyota as well as Mercedes.

When he first took over as CEO, Musk saw the biggest problem related to the widespread adoption of the electric car to be its general limitations when it comes to extended travel. Regardless of the size of the battery, if there are concerns of how you are going to charge when you get where you are going, then the electric car will never be anything more than a novelty. As such, for the past decade, this initiative has increased the number of charging stations that are currently available by more than 300 percent.

This initiative is partially funded by the company SolarCity, also known as the largest supplier of solar energy in all of California. Coincidentally, Musk is also the chairman of the board of this company and is in fact  the reason for its existence. Back in the early 1990s, two of Musk's cousins asked him what a reliable new technology to invest in might be, they were interested in moving to California. Musk told them to consider solar energy and they followed his advice the next year. Their company was the largest supplier of solar energy in all of California by 2007.

Proving again that he has the interests of the world, not just his pocketbook, at heart, Musk has also released all of the patents related to Tesla's electric motor technology in an open source fashion which means that if you have the inclination to build your own electric car, Elon Musk can show you how. Publicly he has explained that this is because he is about promoting the use of electric cars in general, regardless of which company produces them. Currently, Musk's salary with the company is just $1 with anything else being generated from stock options and performance bonuses.

## Moving forward

2017 was an interesting year for Tesla, as it was the first year that the company has really had to face the sheer scope of a project the size of mass production of a (relatively) cheap electric car, the Model 3 electric sedan. While early in the year Musk proudly stated that his company would be producing 5,000 cars per week by the end of the year, December 2017 saw numbers that were about half that. This, after a fall quarter that saw the company losing as much as a million dollars a day where production was first getting started, means that the Model 3 sedan is a gamble roughly on par with the third SpaceX launch when it comes to the long-term viability of the company in its current form.

So far, however, investors remain enthused by the prospect of being a part of the first new successful automaker in the United States in more than 100 years. In fact, the second half of 2017 marked a point where Tesla was, albeit briefly, surpassed General Motors as the auto company in the US with the highest market cap with shares trading near $400 in September. As of February 2018, the two companies are neck in neck, with General Motors being worth just over $59 billion and Tesla being worth just over $53 billion.

While all of the specifics regarding the production of the Model 3 are being kept relatively under wraps, Musk has mentioned publicly that the company has hit significant bottlenecks when it comes to production, though the same could have been said for early models during the initial production stages as well. Part of this is being blamed on an unspecified supplier that failed to live up to early promises resulting in a shortage of project critical lithium batteries. Additionally, Musk has implied that there has been significant difficulty working all of the bugs out of the automated systems that are in place to build the Model 3 which has led to a severely decreased output.

Once the issues with the Model 3 have been sorted out, Musk has already announced that the next vehicle in the Tesla line will be a crossover SUV and has also dropped hints that the project after that he is already dreaming up is going to be an electric pickup truck. Even if the Model 3 doesn't reach its production goals in 2018, it is far too early to count Tesla out of the game, especially considering Musk's track record. That, and the fact that analysts estimate that the company currently has about $1 billion in liquid capital which means they can afford another few supremely unprofitable months before they have to consider looking for additional investor capital.

# CHAPTER 6.

# LOOKING TOWARDS THE FUTURE

When he was in college, Musk asked himself what technologies were likely going to change the world in the next 20 years and then went to work on maximizing his odds of profiting from all of them while at the same time expanding their use and improving on it for the common man. As a Tesla Roadster will soon be orbiting Mars playing David Bowie's Space Oddity, it is safe to say that he has exceeded in spades. This doesn't mean he is finally ready to sit back and take it easy for once, however, as he is already working on a host of other projects that are designed to ensure he leaves the world a far better place than where it was when he found it.

## Hyperloop

In 2013, the state of California was hard at work on a new

high-speed rail system that would run between Los Angeles and San Francisco. It is unclear what Musk was expecting when he went to a meeting for the project, but it is clear that he didn't think California's engineers had developed anything all that great as he felt the need to come up with something better. To make this sudden dream a reality, he pulled together the engineers from Tesla and the engineers from SpaceX and let them work together until they came up with something that was truly high speed.

The result is the Hyperloop, a new form of mass transportation that pushes capsules along at 700 miles per hour on cushions of air. The prototype design for the Hyperloop took the engineer's roughly 12 months to come up with, and once they were completed Musk released them to the public in an open source fashion as well. Still not content, he then announced an open competition for engineers from around the world to develop the best pod to use with the system. Teams can test their designs on a massive test track that Tesla built in California specifically for this purpose.

Additionally, the project is currently in the process of selecting its first public test city route including Columbus-Chicago-Pittsburgh, Dallas-Laredo-Houston; Cheyenne-

Denver-Pueblo, and; Miami-Orlando. Non-U.S. finalists include Toronto-Montreal; Mexico City-Guadalajara; Edinburgh-London; Mumbai-Chennai, and; Bengaluru-Chennai. Each of these projects is expected to save commuters thousands of hours per year by cutting down the amount of time required to travel to central hubs significantly. For example, riders would be able to make it from Columbus Ohio to Chicago Illinois in under half an hour. These finalists were selected from more than 2,600 public-private partnerships from more than 100 countries that applied for a spot among the final 10.

## Open AI

In 2015, Musk created yet another initiative that was designed to help humanity deal with problems that most people weren't even thinking about yet. Specifically, this nonprofit organization is dedicated to creating and researching artificial intelligence in such a way that it evolves in ways that are beneficial and safe for all involved. Musk has stated that he wants the organization to stand against any potential abuse of the masses that could be perpetrated by an artificial intelligence that is created for such a purpose either by a major corporation or world government. OpenAI states that "It's hard to fathom how much human-level AI could benefit society," and that it's equally difficult to comprehend "how much it could damage society if built or used incorrectly"

This nonprofit isn't headed by Musk alone, he has also gathered together other heavy hitters in the genius space including Stephen Hawking and other scientists who believe that artificial intelligence likely poses one of the greatest real-world dangers when it comes to humanity's survival in the long-term. This is the sole reason that Open AI exists, to make sure that artificial intelligence benefits mankind rather than destroys it. While it may seem surprising, the goal is to make artificial intelligence so commonplace that no one person or organization, or AI itself will be able to use what it can do as a means of ending life on the planet as we know it.

As with all of his other projects, the technological breakthroughs that come along with Open AI are all open-source and readily available. Musk is the co-chair of the project and is confident that the organization can stick to its goals without worrying about creating that which they are most afraid of.

Musk has further gone on record as saying that the best way to ensure that artificial intelligence doesn't pose a real threat in the future is to ensure that enough information is readily available and that programming skills are widespread enough to ensure that everyone has the tools they need to protect themselves if things end up getting out of hand. The theory here is that it would be impossible to use an AI to become a world power if they were everywhere in a benign fashion.

In 2017, in an effort to develop more effective ways of learning about artificial intelligence, specifically the ways it can teach itself, the Open AI team started releasing versions of the learning algorithms that are internal artificial intelligence is using. Traditionally, these types of algorithms are generated by throwing huge amounts of data at the machine as the AI is trained to learn based purely on the raw input it receives. The new and improved Open AI, algorithms, however, focus on limiting the number of steps that are realistically required in order for the AI to successfully interact with its environment.

Essentially what this means is that the Open AI artificial intelligence can learn in much the same way that the human brain does. This new programming was put to the test publicly in the summer of 2017 when the Open AI artificial intelligence played against one of the best one of the world's best eSports players at the 2017 Dota 2 International. For reference, the prize pool of the tournament was more than $20 million and the player that competed against the AI has previously taken home nearly a million dollars from tournaments. Their game lasted only a matter of minutes with the artificial intelligence taking out the human player multiple times in a row.

It took the artificial intelligence about two weeks to master one of the most complex video games on the planet to a level greater than any human mind could manage. The goal for the team is to build on this success with even more complex software that will allow future artificial intelligence to learn how to do things such as perform surgery, simply by practicing the required tasks incredibly rapidly.

While the goal of the nonprofit is to create an intelligence that surpasses that of its creators, Musk doesn't believe this is going to happen for a quarter of a century or more. The project will still be going strong at that point as private investors from around the world have already funded it with more than a $1 billion to ensure that its coffers remain full for years to come. Artificial intelligence is the one bet that Musk has made so far that is yet to come true and it appears as though no one, anywhere in the world, is willing to bet against him.

While its first few years of operation saw the organization operate with more or less the same team, 2018 seems to be the year that they are expanding in a big way. Based on the job posting that became available in January 2018, the nonprofit is hiring a recruitment coordinator in hopes of staffing up more significantly in the relatively near future. The Open AI team currently consists of about 60 full-time engineers and researchers who are, according to the job posting, "Working towards their mission regardless of the opportunities for selfish gain which arise along the way."

# CHAPTER 7.

# LESSONS TO LEARN FROM ELON MUSK

As with the great innovators of any age, if you look at the way that Elon Musk has lived his life up to this point you can find a wide variety of lessons that you can easily apply to your own life. It doesn't take much effort to find lessons worth emulating in the life of Elon Musk, and putting them to work on a personal level can make it easier to believe in yourself and to follow your dreams both in the short and the long term.

*Watch for the right time to strike and act when the time is right:* While it can be easy to look at Musk and think that he is successful because he is exceedingly smart and increasingly wealthy, but the truth of the matter is that this is doing the man a disservice. The truth of the matter is that he has reached his current level of success because while in college he took the time to look around and come to the correct conclusions about where things were heading. These indicators were there for anyone to see, and many did, but Musk executed on them in a way that few others could match. First the internet, then space, then electric cars, the same information was out there for anyone else to see, but it took Musk to interpret them correctly and put them to good use.

Musk took a look around him, saw the writing on the wall and then did everything in his power to ensure that he was where he needed to be to take advantage of the situation to the greatest extent possible. More importantly, he didn't let the fact that the odds were against him or that the going was going to be tough dissuade him from following through on his goals. Being insightful is nice, being hardworking is sure to come in handy and being dedicated to a cause makes it easier to follow through, but you really need a combination of all three and an understanding of how to best apply them if you hope to be truly successful in the long run.

*Don't give up:* When looking at Musk's achievements over the years, it can be easy to look at the high points and disregard the times that many people would have given up and taken the easy way out. Don't forget, when he was a child he was almost beaten to death by bullies. As an adult he was forcibly extricated from two different companies that he helped start, it happened at Zip2 and again at PayPal. SpaceX succeeded at the last possible moment and the first version of the vehicle he spent years of his life creating was, by most accounts, an utter failure.

Musk could have dropped out of school rather than face years of bullying or retired after either of his companies was purchased with enough money to keep most people happy for two or three lifetimes. When SpaceX was on the rocks he could have decided on safer investments and after the poor reviews of the Roadster he could have closed down the company and focused on any one of his other successful projects. Instead, he took each of these setbacks in stride and then used them to continue to push himself forward into new and previously unexpected heights. The lesson here should be clear, the things that happen to you don't matter nearly as much as the way you respond to them. The event that breaks one person completely could be just the thing someone else needs to push them on towards greatness. Take each setback as a call to action and you will never stop reaching for new heights.

*Innovation is key:* From the moment that Musk combined a database of business addresses with an online map he has been innovating in any market space he finds himself in which likely explains much of his success. At X.com he could have simply decided to focus on peer-based email transactions, and the world could be using some other payment service besides PayPal or he could have paid $21 million for a single rocket and never gone on to create SpaceX. He could have been content to invest in Tesla without getting actively involved or gone to the California public transportation meeting and thought the speed that was being proposed was good enough.

Instead of being content with the way the world around him currently works, he has always been on the lookout for the flaws inherent in the system that most people ignore and working for ways to turn good enough into great. The lesson here should be obvious, never accept anything less than exactly what you want in the business world. If you can't find what you want, then go ahead and create something new. If you never stop innovating on the success, you have already had then there is no reason to assume that you will ever stop being successful. While the path to innovation might be more difficult than a path based on following the success of others, you will find it far more rewarding in the long run.

*Don't be afraid to put in the work:* Musk is currently the acting CEO for both Tesla Motors and SpaceX, two companies that are each currently worth more than $1 billion each and he has multiple decades' worth of reputation built up for being extremely into micro managing. He is also chairman or co-chair of numerous other boards, head of numerous charities and known to regularly work 100 hours per week. This is because, in his own words, "If you work twice as hard as everyone else then you will get three times as much done each year." With this type of attitude, it doesn't take much to see that hard work and perseverance are the true backbone of his success.

*Find a purpose:* When he was 18, Musk was already musing about electric cars and in his early 20s he was considering the ways he could help humanity get back to space. Furthermore, SpaceX was specifically formed to give humanity a reason to look to the stars with the goal of saving everyone from an extinction level event. Musk doesn't do small dreams or partial solutions when he believes he is following the right path he goes all in and follows that dream to completion.

What this means for those who are trying to follow in his footsteps is that if you ever really want to make those dreams a reality then one of the first things you need to do is take the time to have a heart to heart with yourself and consider if the path you are currently following is the one you are ultimately meant to follow. If this doesn't seem as though it is the case then you need to take a long, hard look at your life and consider where you can make changes that will bring you more in line with whatever it feels as though you were really meant to do. Once you truly start working towards your real purpose you will find that it is far more difficult for anything to really get in your way of making your dream a reality.

*Be open to change:* Just because you have a plan in mind doesn't mean that you shouldn't be open to the possibility that things may change in the future. For example, if Musk remained set in his ways than he would have simply purchased a Russian rocket instead of running the numbers on building his own and stumbling upon a golden opportunity to revitalize interest in space exploration in the process. Likewise, while he obviously had no desire to enact massive layoffs at Tesla, but it was the only way to save the company as a whole.

If he hadn't been open to difficult possibilities, then it is entirely possible that the company would have gone under instead of eventually going on to be worth more than $1 billion as it is today. This just goes to show the importance of rolling with the punches and having the tenacity to do what needs to be done, regardless of the difficulty of the task ahead of you, if you ever hope to truly reach your dreams.

*Don't let others define your success:* When Zip2 was sold to Compaq for $300 million, it dwarfed the sale price of any dotcom company that had come before it. For 99 percent of people out there, that would have been enough success to last the family line for generations. For Musk, however, the company was still a failure because it never lived up to the full potential of its technology that he saw for it in his head. This desire to see the best in the things he creates drown him to see a huge success as a relative failure, which drove him to even greater heights as a result. If you ever hope to follow in his footsteps, this means not letting the way that other people define success or failure determines your own personal outlook on life.

# CHAPTER 8.

# ELON MUSK IN HIS OWN WORDS

*Life Philosophy: ['But you were willing to bet the farm on this (space travel) Conversation with Elon Musk Kahn academy April 2013.* "Yeah, I figured like I was willing to spend half the money I got from PayPal on this with no expectation of success. because I thought that was just something that was pretty important, and yeah, I'm like, it seems like I can spend half the money I got from PayPal on this, and it would be, if that got NASA a bigger budget that resulted in going to Mars, then that would be a pretty good outcome."-Elon Musk

*Knowledge: [How did a degree help?] Stanford University Entrepreneurial Thought Leaders Conference October 2003.*

"I think for instance teachers with a lot of the terminology, introduces you to concepts that you would otherwise, there's terminology there's something to be said for that, introduces you to concepts you would otherwise have to learn empirically.

I mean I think you can learn whatever you need to do to start a successful business either in school or out of school. A school, in theory, should help accelerate that process and I think oftentimes it does. It can be an effective learning process, perhaps more efficient than empirically learning lessons. I mean there are examples of successful entrepreneurs who never graduated high school and there are those that have PhDs. So, I think the important principle is to be dedicated to learning what you need to know, whether that is in school or empirically."- Elon Musk

*Life Philosophy: [Question about future projects and failure.] The Future of Energy and Transport November 2012.* "I think I'm going to stay on electric cars and rockets for a while. It was actually never my intent to run Tesla, because running two companies is quite a burden, actually. I sometimes run into people who think, oh, if you're CEO of the company then they sort of imagine themselves, if they were CEO of the company, they would grant themselves lots of vacation and do lots of fun things.

It's doesn't quite work that way. What you actually get is, a distillation of the worst things going on in the company. So, the idea of taking on something more is very frightening. Possibly, at some point in the future, certainly not the near term, there's an opportunity to create an electric jet, eventually. I do think I want to create an electric jet that is really exciting.

Something that would be supersonic, vertical takeoff and landing, pure electric, and just a big leap forward. I'm quite confident it's doable, provided that there's a rough doubling of the energy density in batteries or capacitors. Basically, around the 500W/kg level is where it starts to make sense. I do think there's the possibility of a fifth mode of transport which I've mentioned tangentially, which I call the Hyperloop.

I'd like to publish something about that, maybe in the next month or two, once Tesla is at steady state production, and I want to flesh it out a bit so that I can pre-address some of the rebuttals that people will come up with, rather than just put it out there and then have the rebuttal occur and have an unaddressed rebuttal. I guess a way to think of it is, it's like a cross between a Concorde and a rail gun."-Elon Musk

*Success: [Can you talk a little bit about the difference in the customer base you have targeted in SpaceX that enforces experiences with PayPal how much challenge that presents?] Stanford University Entrepreneurial Thought Leaders Conference October 2003.* "Yes. The customer base with SpaceX is dramatically different obviously from PayPal. PayPal is a consumer product whereas SpaceX we're selling rockets and the number of people who want to buy rockets is quite small. If anyone here has explained to everyone a rocket, I'd be glad to sell it to him. So, it's much more of an individual selling process.

There's a great deal more thought that goes to any purchase of a launch, much more so that signing up a PayPal account which doesn't really cost you much, and there's not a lot of viral marketing that's going to happen with a rocket I suspect. I'm hoping but I'm not counting on it.

I think successful entrepreneurs probably come in all sizes, shapes and flavors. I'm not sure there's any one particular thing. For me, some of the things I've described already I think are very important. I think really an obsessive nature with respect to the quality of the product is very important and so being an obsessive-compulsive is a good thing in this context.

Really liking what you do, whatever area that you get into, even if you're the best of the best, there's always a chance of failure so I think it's important that you really like whatever you're doing. If you don't like it, life is too short. I'd say also if you like what you're doing, you think about it even when you're not working. It's something that your mind is drawn to and if you don't like it, you just really can't make it work I think.

*Motivation: [Question about outsourcing] Q&A Session at the University of California in March of 2011.* "Businesses sometimes tend to be a little sort of fad-y. For a very long time there was a very strong outsourcing fad. But I don't think people really looked at the fundamentals in a lot of cases when they outsourced. Particularly when the technology is developing rapidly, it's important to have a very tight iteration loop between engineering and production, so as soon as you design something you can bring it to production right away.

And the engineers can go on the floor and see the mistakes that they've made, the production people can talk to engineers and say, 'here are some good ideas,' and so you can evolve the product and get to a better design solution faster. I think this is an important thing that's often overlooked.

At SpaceX our rockets are lower cost than the Chinese, the Indians, anyone else, and that's before reusability is taken into account. I think it's largely because of that tight iteration loop."- Elon Musk

*Creating a company [USC Commencement Speech]:* "The other thing I'd say is that if you're creating a company, or if you're joining a company, the most important thing is to attract great people. So, either be with, join a group that's amazing, that you really respect. Or, if you're building a company, you've got to gather great people. I mean, all a company is a group of people that have gathered together to create a product or service. So, depending upon how talented and hardworking that group is, and to the degree in which they are focused cohesively in a good direction, that will determine the success of the company. So, does everything you can to gather great people, if you're creating a company.

Then, I'd say focus on signal over noise. A lot of companies get confused.

They spend a lot of money on things that don't actually make the product better.

So, for example, at Tesla, we've never spent any money on advertising.

We've put all the money into R and D and manufacturing and design to try and make the car as good as possible. And, I think that's the way to go. For any given company, keep thinking about, "Are, these efforts that people are expending, are they resulting in a better product or service?"

And if they're not, stop those efforts.

And then the final thing is, is to sort of, don't just follow the trend.

So, you may have heard me say that it's good to think in terms of the physics approach, the first principles. Rather than reasoning by analogy.

If you boil things down to the most fundamental truths you can imagine, and then you reason up from there. And this is a good way to figure out if something really makes sense or is it just what everybody else is doing.

It's hard to think that way, you can't think that way about everything.

It takes a lot of effort. But if you're trying to do something new, it's the best way to think. And that framework was developed by physicists to figure out counter intuitive things, like quantum mechanics. It's really a powerful, powerful method. -Elon Musk

*Dealing with fear [December 2017 interview]:* Starting a company is like staring at the abyss and eating glass, and there's some truth to that. The staring into the abyss part is that you are going to be constantly facing the extermination of the company, because most start-ups fail. It's like 90% ~ 99% of start-ups fail. That's the staring into the abyss part. You're constantly saying, "If I don't get this right, the company will die." Which can be quite stressful.

The eating glass part is, you've got to work on the problems that the company needs you to work on, not the problems you want to work on. So, you end up working on problems that you really wish you weren't working on, so that's the eating glass part.

On the big picture, you know where you're generally heading for, and the actual path is going to be some sort of zig-zaggy thing in that direction. Try not to deviate too far from the path that you want to be on, but you're going to have to do that to some degree.

You'll hear something, "Well, I feel fear about this, and therefore I shouldn't do it." It's normal to feel fear. There would have to be something mentally wrong if you didn't feel fear. I feel it quite strongly. But there are just times when something is important enough, you believe in it enough that you do it in spite of the fear. – Elon Musk

*On Mankind's future [ Caltech commencement speech 2012]:* So, it's really somewhat of a tenuous existence that civilization and consciousness has been on earth. I'm actually fairly optimistic about the future earth. I don't want to give the wrong impression like we're all about to die. [Laughter] I think things will be okay for a long time on earth. Not for sure, but, most likely. But even if it's 99% likely, a 1% chance is still worth the effort to back up the biosphere and achieved planetary redundancy. And I think it's really quite important.

And in order to do that, there's great things that are needing to occur. Create a rapidly reusable transport system to Mars. It's something right on the borderline of impossible. But, that's the sort of the thing that we're going to try to achieve with SpaceX. -Elon Musk

*On artificial intelligence [2017 interview]:* In my opinion, the biggest risk that we face as a civilization, is artificial intelligence. Last year AlphaGo, which was done by DeepMind, which is kind of a Google subsidiary, absolutely crushed the world's best player. Now it can play at the top 50 simultaneously and crush them all. Just that pace of progress is remarkable, and you can see more and more coming up. Like the robotics, you can see robots that can learn to walk from nothing, you know within hours. Way faster than any biological being.

The thing that's most dangerous is, and it's the hardest to kind of get your arms around because it's not a physical thing, is kind of a deep intelligence in the network. You say, well what harm could a deep intelligence in the network do? Well, it could start a war by doing fake news, and spoofing email accounts, and fake press releases, and just by manipulating information. The pen is mightier than the sword. - Elon Musk

# CONCLUSION

Thank you for making it through to the end of *The Future Is Now: How Elon Musk Is Shaping A Better Tomorrow*, let's hope it was informative and able to provide you with all of the tools you need to not only understand the many potentially life altering things that Elon Musk has already accomplished but use his example to improve your own lot in life as well.

While it can be easy to idolize the people who are actively working to make the world a better place, and assume that they naturally selected by destiny to be special, this mindset does them, as well as you a disservice. The fact of the matter is that they were able to get to where they are today through hard work and determination and your assumption that they are special minimizes the impressiveness of the things they have accomplished. Instead of blind hero worship, it is far more productive to look at them with an eye towards the things they are doing that their competition is not.

Additionally, while it is true that Musk is likely naturally smarter than you, there are literally dozens of other things he has done you can take to heart, that have nothing to do with your natural level of intelligence. After all, taking a look at your circumstances and coming up with the best course of action from there is something that anyone can do. After all, it doesn't take a genius to understand that by working harder than your competition you can see better results. Rather than assuming those who are truly successful just have something that you lack. It is far more productive to look at the things they have done to reach success and consider the ways that you can follow in their footsteps.

Finally, if you found this book useful in any way, a review on Amazon is always appreciated!

www.ingramcontent.com/pod-product-compliance
Lightning Source LLC
Chambersburg PA
CBHW051841250726
48659CB00005B/1969